BEHIND THE SCENES BIOGRAPHIES

WHAT YOU NEVER KNEW ABOUT

ADDISON RAE

by Mari Schuh

CAPSTONE PRESS
a capstone imprint

This is an unauthorized biography.

Published by Spark, an imprint of Capstone
1710 Roe Crest Drive, North Mankato, Minnesota 56003
capstonepub.com

Library of Congress Cataloging-in-Publication Data
is available on the Library of Congress website.
ISBN: 9798875210440 (hardcover)
ISBN: 9798875210396 (paperback)
ISBN: 9798875210402 (ebook PDF)

Summary: Addison Rae has millions of followers on TikTok. She's starred on the
big screen. But what is her life like behind the scenes? What are some of her
little-known talents? What job did she want to have before becoming a social
media star? These questions and more will be answered in this high-interest,
carefully leveled book that will enthrall reluctant and struggling readers.

Editorial Credits
Editor: Carrie Sheely; Designer: Elijah Blue; Media Researcher: Jo Miller;
Production Specialist: Tori Abraham

Image Credits
Alamy: Abaca Press , 7, tofino, 13; Getty Images: Frazer Harrison, 12, 14, Jay
L. Clendenin, 8, Kevin Mazur/MG22, 20, Kevin Winter, 22, Matt Winkelmeyer,
cover, Rachpoot/Bauer-Griffin, 17, 24, Roger Kisby, 4, Stewart Cook, 19, Theo
Wargo, 28, Vittorio Zunino Celotto, 27; Los Angeles Times via Getty Images,
9; Shutterstock: Berkahlineart, 15, Christos Georghiou, 16, Featureflash
Photo Agency, 11, grey_and, 5 (basketball), Joseph Hendrickson, 25 (Jeep),
kumakumalatte, 23 (both), mhatzapa, 25 (fruit), Tanya Sid, 5 (toilet)

Design Elements: Shutterstock: Illerlok_xolms

Printed and bound in China. 006276

TABLE OF CONTENTS

Words in **bold** are in the glossary.

SOCIAL MEDIA
STAR

Addison Rae is one of TikTok's biggest stars. Being a star means she gets to be a guest on fun TV shows. On one show, she and the host made sandwiches in the host's bathroom. They also ate ice cream and played basketball there!

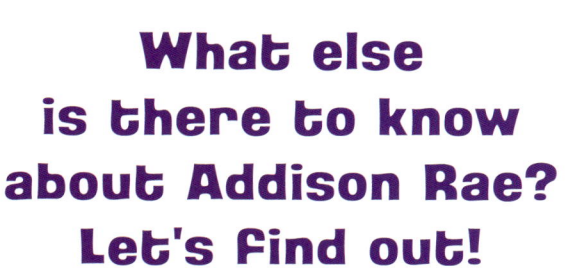

What else is there to know about Addison Rae? Let's find out!

ADDISON'S
LIKES

How much do you know about Addison? Test your knowledge!

1. **Favorite color?**

2. **Favorite book series?**

3. **Favorite foods?**

4. **Favorite dessert?**

5. **Favorite go-to makeup item?**

6. **Bonus points for the superpower Addison wants the most!**

1. Deep purple   2. *Pretty Little Liars*

3. Bananas and peanut butter   4. Anything matcha

5. Mascara   6. To speak every language in the world

ADDISON
BY THE NUMBERS

Addison was born October 6, 2000. Her full name is Addison Rae Easterling. In 2014, she joined Instagram at age 14. Addison was 19 years old when she posted her first video on TikTok in 2019. In just a few months, she had 1 million followers!

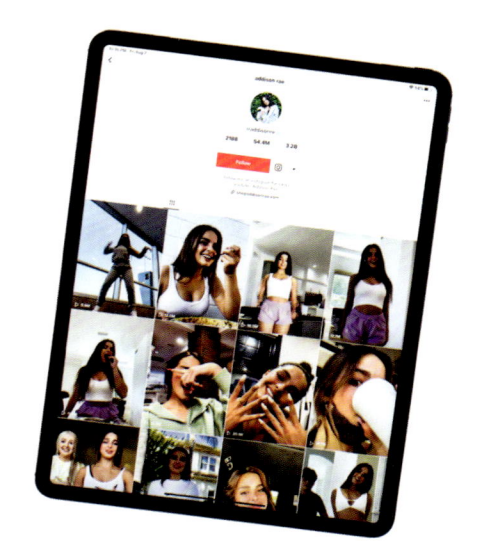

FACT

Addison's first video to get 1 million likes had her mom in it.

Addison dances and **lip-synchs** on **social media**. People love her posts. She has more than 88 million followers on TikTok. Those followers have given her 5.8 billion likes!

Addison is popular on other sites too. More than 35 million people follow her on Instagram. On YouTube, she has 4.2 million subscribers. Addison is also popular on X, where she has 4.6 million followers.

FACT

In 2021, Addison won a Streamy Award. The awards recognize online video creators.

GROWING **UP**

Growing up, Addison was a fan of MTV. She spent hours watching the TV channel's music videos. Then she would make her own music videos in her bedroom. She dreamed of being a big star one day!

FACT

Addison has been dancing since she was about 6. She danced in competitions around the U.S.

Addison with her dad, Monty Lopez, her mom, Sheri Easterling, and her two brothers

Addison loves roller coasters. When she was a child, she and her dad had lots of fun riding roller coasters together. Her dad believed the exciting rides could help Addison. How? The fast roller coasters could help her face her fears.

It seems like Addison is always on the go. Addison was very busy before she became a huge social media **influencer** too! In high school, Addison loved to do gymnastics. She was also a cheerleader.

BRANCHING OUT

Addison's massive fame reaches beyond social media. She's a rising movie star on the big screen. As a singer, she's becoming known for her pop music. In 2020, she was the voice of Marnie in the **animated** movie *Spy Cat*.

FACT
Addison played the character Gabby in the 2023 movie *Thanksgiving*.

Sniff Sniff

What's that sweet scent? In 2021, Addison was excited to take a little break from her smartphone. Why? She helped create her own line of fragrances. The bottles change color based on the temperature of their surroundings. How sweet is that?

ADDISON'S **WORLD**

Addison is known for being happy, positive, and cheery. But she isn't shy about letting fans know she feels other **emotions**, just like they do. Mean comments that people post about her on social media can make her sad. She also gets nervous before her songs are released.

Addison loves fast, colorful cars. In 2020, she bought a Tesla Model X. The car got a bubble-gum pink **wrap** added to it. The car matched her pink cowboy hat. She gave the car a hug the first time she saw it. When it was time for something different, Addison had the car's color changed to navy blue.

FACT

Addison also owns a Jeep Wrangler that has fruit painted on it.

ADDISON
TRUE OR FALSE

1. Mountains are Addison's favorite outdoor scenery.

2. Addison starred in a candy commercial.

3. Addison can juggle fruit.

4. Addison has appeared on the TV show *Keeping Up with the Kardashians.*

5. Addison wanted to be a teacher.

1. FALSE (Addison prefers the beach.)   **2.** TRUE (She was in a Nerds candy commercial that aired during the 2024 Super Bowl.)   **3.** TRUE

4. TRUE   **5.** FALSE (She wanted to be a sports broadcaster.)

HELPING OTHERS

Addison uses her star power to help others. In 2020, she and tennis player Taylor Fritz won $1 million in an online gaming **charity** tournament. She donated the money to help feed children. In 2022, she helped raise money for people with cancer. Addison is a big star who makes a big difference!

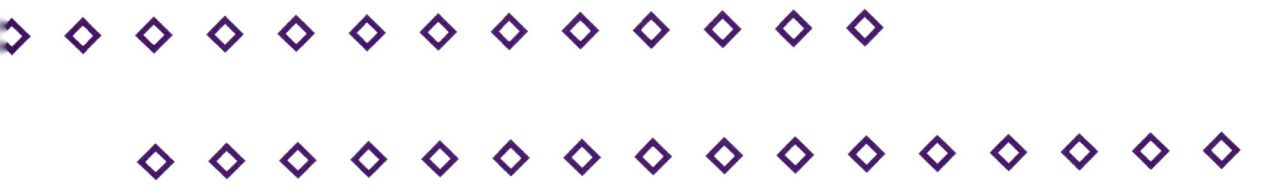

Glossary

animated (a-nuh-MAY-tud)—a long recording of cartoons made by quickly presenting drawings, one after another, so that the characters seem to be moving

charity (CHAYR-uh-tee)—a group that raises money or collects goods to help people in need

emotion (i-MOH-shuhn)—a strong feeling; people have and show emotions such as happiness, sadness, fear, anger, and jealousy

influencer (IN-floo-uhnss-er)—a person who has an effect on someone

lip-synch (LIP SINK)—to pretend to sing at the same time a song is playing

social media (SOH-shul MEE-dee-uh)—websites, apps, and games that connect people as they share photos, videos, and other content; TikTok, Instagram, and X are popular social media platforms

wrap (RAP)—a vinyl covering on a vehicle

Read More

Braun, Eric. *Can You Become a Social Media Influencer?: An Interactive Adventure*. North Mankato, MN: Capstone, 2022.

Brian, Rachel. *Screen Time!* New York: Little, Brown and Company, 2024.

Green, Sara. *TikTok*. Minneapolis: Bellwether Media, Inc., 2024.

Internet Sites

Beano: Epic Addison Rae Quiz
beano.com/posts/ultimate-addison-rae-quiz

IMDb: Addison Rae Biography
imdb.com/name/nm11290905/bio

Kiddle: Addison Rae Facts for Kids
kids.kiddle.co/Addison_Rae

Index

About the Author

Mari Schuh's love of reading began with cereal boxes at the kitchen table. Today, she is the author of hundreds of nonfiction books for beginning readers. Mari lives in the Midwest with her husband and their sassy house rabbit. Learn more about her at marischuh.com.